The Mojo Hands
Call/I Must Go

the Mojo Hands Call, I Must Go

Sterling D. Plumpp

THUNDERS MOUTH PRESS   1982   NEW YORK   CHICAGO

Copyright © 1982 Thunde

All rights reserved under I
Pan American Copyright C

Published in the United Sta
Mouth Press, 242 W 104th
York, NY 10025 and Box
IL 60611.

Design by Ray Machura

Acknowledgment is gratefu
following magazines, in wh
book originally appeared, a
who have issued some of th
separate volumes.

Another Chicago Magazine: '
Dreams," "The Mojo Hands Call/I Must Go
Broadside Press: *Clinton*
Obsidian: "I Hear the Shuffle of the
People's Feet"
Savage: "Clinton" (in a slightly different version)
Third World Press: *Steps to Break the Circle*,
"Sugar Woman" (in *Portable Soul*)

Library of Congress Cataloging in
Publication Data:

Plumpp, Sterling, 1940-
The Mojo hands call, I must go.

I. Title.
PS3566.L79M6 1982 811'.54
82-10360
ISBN 0-938410-04-0 (pbk.)

*for
Harriet Nzinga,
my daughter
and future*

Contents

Sugar Woman

She was black
And we called her sugar.

In the dense briars
Of life's uncertainties,
A pie.

We called her love.

Our sight strengthened
By soft beauty. Our
Manhood moulded in
Her ways.

We called her queen,
(Beautiful black queen
Sugar. . . . .
         and mother.

Fractured Dreams

1   do i walk the streets alone
burdened like a memory limping in the head
age-pushed in shadows
i once wrapped our day; confronted
with echoes of yesterday's harvest?

do i walk streets
on soured dreams/opened in the air of insomnia?
is there night shaved hostility
bordered beyond my steps?

do i walk where there are now vows
bearded on faces/begging
for extra prints to my former paths
a child wingless in flight
on the road beginning
frightened at the noise, unredeemed
by nests nappy in a large certainty
alone
bifocalled in the "ego cell"?

do i walk pensioned memories
rail-like/a mendicant consigned
to executions in eyes
senile in my cloudy trials?
where is the edge of birth
prying against stagnancy/flowers
jimmying fear to free respect?

do i walk chipped stones
hollow from plodding of crippled winds
hoboing ice-clad roads/making
a struggle to see the sun again/hoboing
on the morning that rakes blizzards over my face?
do i walk at this hour/before my day has satisfied
a finitude for its head?

do i walk night/evil in despair
a wretched chill gnawing at the core
of apples our hands meditated into a world?
do i walk sleepless highways
as a fragmented giant stubbing his toe on the dew?

do i walk the streets alone
always
even in my fantasies/barbecued
by muscles bodied in agreement/ripe
fruits swimming in limbo? was there ever
places teeming/where my steps did not talk
splintered tongues? was there ever droves
settled where we made dreams/briefed hope
on coming designs? did i ever walk in confidence/
dancing with the crowd/one
in the many seeds of a new day?

do i walk sounds
the mojo curses sprinkled on my shoes
phantom hands rubbing devilment
on desires of my way? do i walk
hoodoo gravel scattered in pulpits
of funk-fumed meeting houses?

do i walk alone, at night,
bare feet tripping the knife of paranoia
spiders clawing my past
my bones gritted by today's hunger?
do i walk, at night, outside my skin
an exile from within/a comic window
broken by tears of unknown beggars?

do i walk para-deathships/rocking
on indecisions of my hands/screaming
through the end passage/jumping overboard
into drug-silent traps/my soul auctioned
at lids of waves/wretched in their exploitations?
do i walk terror/alone-bred in dissolution
my prayers shedding their steel
like a tree does bark?

do i walk alone/tied in the fog
wading toward a trapdoor? is this
chance or the cyclic view
pushing into my vision? do i walk trails
hound-dogged/a runaway from myself/
my fortune told by winds
as they whistle behind my tracks?

do i walk streets/adrift in chaos
desecrated outposts breeding loneliness?
is my heart the only voice/resonant
against battlefields of chimes? do i walk/
a crumpled page entangled in mud
an absent pupil sawed from knowledge?

do i walk alone/root-starved
a balanced obstacle/sober
on a channel of illusions?
do i walk/a paralytic joke
fumbling on the tongue
a blind image jay-walking
across skulls?

do i walk the streets alone
a cybernetic trickster/an autobiography
whimpering a biographical fragment?
do i walk streets/a self-plea
ragged in jumpsuits of passing dreams?
do i dangle like a participle/lost
from moons showing the archival loot?
are gestures coiled in my loins
rusted by oxides of delirium?

do i walk alone/bent behind caution
a blues song barred from ears
of people's goodtimes/a riff
with its back at the wrong end of a horn/limping
into a cacophony? do i walk/an unkempt boogie
disco-ing on tissued floors of bop
a scrappled be parking at charlie's door?

do i walk/a tipsy shadow gangrening
epithets at his echo
a crystal somersault jiving around
on baldheads of concrete
a boy-rag spit-shining weeds?
do my fathers cringe
because i unveiled their secrets
with apathy, because i twisted courage
so it cannot fit their locks,
because i walk/crowded sirens of a fad?

do they turn over/screening out
indented servitudes of my fear?
do their eyes point talons
of hoot-owl talk at my mind?

do i walk alone/crying dotted fungi
an aborted defiance/peeping one-eyedly
through smoke webs of an ear
a hand-me-down obituary yellowing?
do i walk the streets/pad-lipped by manias
egoed on ancestral voices
a self-definition leaking
an ossified rhythm detained in slow molasses?

do i walk the streets alone
a derailed smile/chinning down the line?
a bow-fingered incompetent gigging
on the bass of nat turner's bones.
do i walk alone/a solitary shoe
perplexed over feet to swim
in his pond?

do i walk the streets alone/because i
shaved manes from the great stallion,
because i emptied the cow, because i am
a dilettante drinking from a griot's gourd,
because i fed my birthright to swines. . . . .

2   can i live
a button-hole sucking the blues tongue
a moonshine epidemic spread
on sandwiches of a moan

can a midget ladder climb
can i live rent-free
a poet up-side-down in vision/reading
tomorrow with a headless pen
an amnesiac stork errant in creation
can i live

can a peg-legged haint escape day
can i live
in ransom notes of poverty
a toad-stool philosopher scraping
bacteria from feeling's rump
can a mood catastrophe
ripen a pregnancy of survival

can a model-t effort bake
sky-scrappered crusts
can i live
weaving on bald tires
a telescopic drifter stationed on dipsomania
can a total-lost incompetent resurrect
in body shops of today's hunger
can i live
a near-sighted tootsie roll shacked up
with concubines of greed
can a black boy live

can i live
a blues bunion squatting on acidic turf
a midnight yell hung from saltine lashes of agony
a gypsy booga training in the nose
can pneumonia wombs
give birth to wheaties's smiles
can a bacculaureate of happiness
bloom from phlegmatic roots
can i live
an imported disgrace/naturalized
by civic lessons in dementia

can i live
petrified guts paper-clipped in museums of terror
a leader articulate in the propaganda of silence
heir to the body politic of leukemia
can a nile boy of menes
swim in Neanderthal pond
an olympic flapjack competing in accomodation
a terrapinic sprinter running for liberation

can a supine slag bench press
skirts of a grinding choo-choo
can i live
a jig-saw tributary whining
for fragments to mother's arms
a pre-fab soldier marching
on iron-girthed regiments
can marginal laughter camoflouge
vulnerability of paraplegic deathblows
can i live

can i live
a nomadic memory sunning
in after thoughts of cacti
a bedouin infidel making salat
on a rug of pig skins

can i live
a makeshift nerve weeping please
can a barren drum
talk music to curses of an alien place

3   the ground hog always sees his shadow.
in my hours
the omen spelling six more deaths
is a long tunnel winter-stretching
into infinity. i forget my minutes
shelacked on sub-zero floors.
i forget xylophonic walks
Bags-steeped in rhythm corners.
i forget the time i had.

beheaded by icicles
my time is a powerless isotope
conked on watchtowers of gold.
my day is eclipsed by mortgages
wise-cracking in studios of foreclosure.
a prologue vagabond, i comply
a meandering character outside his drama.
i comply/frigid scrubbed on roller coasters of sin.
a polar teddy offered as prize
in the carnival of my mind/i comply
a juggernaut failure bob-sledding
down heads of frost.

stalactites, my years droop/frozen
by yelps of blood-hounding glaciers.
every thought is a dried lake
gaping from eyes in my palms.
my soul is wet confetti thumbing a ride
from the proboscis of a wind/a pain managerie
viewed by drizzles of hail troopers.
part of my way/is a philosophical omelet
cloudy-side on arctic toast of darkness.

every second falls/humpty dumpty spills
masquerade in my veins. am i/a genetic conspiracy
self-erasing on spires of an iceberg
a molotov rage slapping walls.
the broken shells scatter/all the stick-pins
cannot set my time again. leprosy sleets
on my spirit. . .

in my hours
an avalanche implosion markets my nerves.
my day is an emaciated echo/prostrate
before the congregation of song.
i ride huskies over nordic poles
to vampiric declensions of drought
a monozide zombie carbon-copied
by anarctic xerox mountains.
i walk the glacial dance/a vapor coward
bootlicking halls of the cosmos
a syphilitic dice rolling losers.

snowmen spur my insides.
their polar fire rides broncos
in rodeos of my memory. i pass time
in a nap sack/a frozen spittoon
hostage to eskimos' vomit freeze
ice stampedes trouble my world
with epochal fall-outs
as hiroshimiric ice-ages snore in my day.
my hours are pig-balloons/inflated
by windy termites. i pollute history
a sty metaphor descending corruption.
i cannot rise/i am jailed
hibernating in anemia

Clinton

1   Before me/taut pallets of smoke.
    Day waking from pores like black smiles
    Defying tenements' grasps. Rural town,
    Your skies got the blues.
    My longings like cigarettes
    Come back for your deep sleepdrags.
    It is inhalation, winged memoryreel
    Of panoramic comfort that takes
    My infancy again to diapers and dust
    In the front yard. The song of flowers
    Breathing windy perfumes agitates
    The fever of sunshine. Escalators.
    Your gullies and hills. I run
    Through rains from tree
    To tree when thunder and lightning
    Lie bedridden. Spring.
    I am looking out/on uncle's shoulders
    Before feet can enroll in your rich embrace.
    Funny. How old and young, men and women,
    Animals and plants, come up with the sun
    To darn the morning with laughter.

2   Talk between the people and the soil
Goes on in sermons by middlebusters
Solos by section harrows
Graces of cultivators
Shouts by swinging hoes
And confessions by hands and knees.
The little plants of cotton, corn, tulip,
Bean, turnip, and okra, open their eyes
To the sun and people bending.
Growth of the vines is a "hello"
Climbing to greet minstrel poles.

3   Night town, strange winds of mystery
Blowing ghosts of rising moons,
I rock in your harvested bosom.
My milk and bread in a bowl
Come through tar-tars from momma.
Hot cornbread crumbles like dirt clods
And makes the clabber bubble.
Before my bowl runs it over
I shovel my spoon to my tummy
And run to the pot before I do-dos
What I gotta do.

4   Dick Tracy chases Eighty-Eight Keys
     Past Little Nancy and Slugo.
     Cotton town, crossroads town
     Of honeysuckle blossoms on fences
     Like the faithful on the King's Highway,
     Work is seed tonic, logical wine
     Committed to the thirsty reason of men
     Winning today's rib tips of command
     With the swallowing of their labors.
     Out cross blackness
     Lightning bugs soul clap with stars.
     In my heart I want sweetwater
     And before I drink at prayer time
     Momma says "She is your momma;
     I am your grandmomma". I could not
     Understand her meaning and my thirst
     Became bitter mosquito bites. Shucks
     In the mattress played hide
     Tickling feathers in the pillow
     So they flapped in my face. I lay
     Listening to snores of unanswering walls.

5   Morning glories
    Pull down music of work days,
    Hometown, straw hat men
    Walk with round women in ginghams.
    I plow unfurrowed rows of my life:
    Swinging in trees, sliding down hillsides,
    And playing in cotton sheds.
    My song of longing leaps
    Through radios of your vistas
    Like instant dreams in cups of sleep.
    The mud and rains of freshness
    Stroke my body like a do-right woman.
    Black folks picking cotton
    Hauling it to gins
    Being cheated and whipped
    Side their heads if complaints
    Burst from sorghum lips.

6   Like a quail
I saunter down your dusty roads
Evenings and dare
Hound your paths, nights
When ghosts blow their cold breaths
In my face when I climb hills
And rinse me in hotness
As I walk in valleys. Rails
Crack with the Bugga Man's steps.
Darkness is a blanket. I touch it.
I cannot sleep anymore unless
My mind exhumes your covers
From the couch of memory.
Momma breaking clods to insert
Seed birth of promised greenness.
Years blink in the distance
Like comets. Yet my scope
Is set on fall afternoons
When leaves wear reddish brown
Shirts and bop to the ground.
Dew comes in mugs of fog
And the sun oversleeps
But goes to bed early.
Off in your nights frost
Becomes coconut of midnight cake
As we watch the simmon tree
For an old possum. . .

7   Today at the edge of light
I soar back to your horizon
Like wise lips hugging thighs.
This hedonistic kneeling of wonder
Yearns in my loins
Dry ice in time's hind pocket.
And I cannot but glory at the sight
Of yesterday rocking down
Through the perversity of my despair
Like an old Black man in a buggy
The bay mare trotting and
He sitting in judgment like Pontius Pilate.
Summer town, I walk out on your fingertips
Reaching for grapes and black cherries.
The bucket I carry in my heart
Is a memory vault. Cotton mouth moccassins,
Spreading adders, and rattlers
Coiling at your toes for granite peace.

8   I resound in your wide halls,
Dirt town, red clay boys
Throwing mudballs
Against banks and one another,
Men and women in rubber boots
Wading and making ditches,
And setting tomatoes and onions straight
On rows. I am pierced by brightness
Of momma's headrag and cleanliness of her apron.
Poppa's overalls are true blue
And patches have conspired
To conceal holes. Autumn.
Pecans rolling around
And hiding under leaves.
I stuff my pockets/eating
Until my belly aches. Castor oil
Invades my ancestral pride
To make my minutes loose.

9   Bad town, I see a white-faced bull
     Snorting anger out his nose and pawing
     With sturdy precision to zero his body in.
     I want to follow a leader beyond clouds
     To high nests. Thickets become my refuge.
     I walk miles in them. Before long I hear
     A bellow coming to the trees. I run
     To our yard and enter the grave/wooden gate.
     With the agony of black widows leaving grave sites/
     Husbands in their eyes, I withdraw to bed
     Being checked by a white face
     And a huffing and a puffing in the ground.

     Night loops of silence/I come to loiter
     A black seed in a ripe watermelon. I sit
     In tribute of backlogs filling cavities in walls
     With rowdy heat. January weekends are great days
     For sitting/talking/roasting/and drinking.
     Jars of peaches are opened on homemade bread.
     Friends and relatives drop by with news.
     Extra plates come with bowls of gumbo.
     Soppings go on in seconds and the cobbler
     Is last to go.

     I trot out in the wild wind.
     Sable coffee of you stencils
     My soul. School/blackboards, benches,
     Tables, and toilets outside. Mrs. Latham
     Sits watching mouths for gum and quick hands
     For spitballs. I cannot go unless
     There is an excuse me. Sumner Hill
     Is white sides and a green top.
     I put my lunch on a desk/then take
     My initial wisdom strokes.

10   I come crying/dry leaves
In the wind. Suddenly back
Where lasses and cornbread are vows
Wedded to butter. A looking-glass
Reflects hours/sassysweet dust kissed rains
In times I hugged tight over potlicker.
Could it be/now I am away/far and older/
That joy I know is but a breeze
From clarinets swaying in ways
Only Al Green can feel to order
With his inside love screams?

I have known the arresting
Tender surrender of leaves and
Sap piping green monsoons on desire.
Have known my life is music baked
By fingers only Max-Roached-Monks
Taking C-Tranes can buy with salt peanuts
Of insight. My growing years gallop
Like hoofs of justice. Fear rides
In my veins/when I am jailed by Jim Crow/
When I remember Willie McGhee burning/
Remember Emmett Till drowning/when I remember
Those castrated by silent consent
Not to revel in songs of their manhood.

I sing in solitude; sing pouring
Ways into your gourds and I drink
Recognition. I sing to Holy Ghost
Years/Sumner Hill's diction in accents.
Daily immersion into what St. Thomas said
He thought God was all about and
Life supposed to be. My neck bending
From beads/rosaries saying any life
Without the Roman seal is lost.

11 What is this hip yearning smooching hot
In my breath with passion cut by young
Southern language? What is my life
But a little cup of knowledge? What is
Pain joy sadness love happiness
And despair but a gumbo of life simmering
In pots of your wonder days, nightchild town?
The winds and ways people move
Are scars drawn on your morning valley face
By diasporic singers crying holy blues.
Your lips bless my presence with Satchmo's
Embouchure, small town.

Where do the past's fingers end?
Is yesterday but today and tomorrow
Called in more intimate poetry?
Where is the when of this angling statue
Carved in man's memory as footprints
Of events loved? Where is your magnolia sweetness
To zip up my mind? The streets wind in tune
With pathologies. Crimes manufactured
From need. Songs blown by life. I uncover
Your legacy in the city. Death paints my reality
Before I can pull sounds into sonic graffitti.

12   Your morning peace still drums
Color into Chicago's climate. I go
From open diaries. High school with nuns
Bunnied up in blue. Boys and girls
From "better classes" riding bicycles
And thinking they in space ships
To power and wealth. I am lost.
Keeping somebody else's seven sacraments.
Worshipping fear. Running from everything real.
College is no better than grammar school
Or high school. Only signs of illness
Are less visible. I am in an asylum.
Poor light. Strangers block mirrors
And muddy the water. Songs I have
Drown in books. I am condemned
To repeat names of the dead.

Chicago. Winds bandaging wounds
On faces. Making the world go mad.
My campus after St. Benedict's rules
Tried to commit me behind bars forever.
Ten-hour days. Mail bags. People working
And drifting in confusion. Men fighting
Men. Letting the boy kick their asses
And keep them humping till their number
To move up on the plantation is pulled.

Vision is all life can ever be. Man rising
From clay to control the stars
Because he covets his shadow hovering
In clear days. My source. You are vision.
Back down in Mississippi. Vision. This thunder
Pounding in the music I live.

13   The army. I cannot even dream.
     My vision so fixated on suffering
     I nearly lose songs spread across decades
     My steps took to ripen a music
     That is sight. Vision/I say
     Is all a poet is and all life is.
     Vision is all I could hold onto.
     I wake. Morning calling me/notes bopping
     Blue and mighty loud in make believe soldiers
     Grinding their lives in rinds. Marching
     To whistles monsters are blowing.
     And the sky is grey and crying. I rise
     From government issued hurt laughing.
     Tears walking down my face.

     The world. A womb and I, bottled flesh,
     Dependent upon land to uncork my soul.
     Every thought I imagine is thrown
     By hands of the land. That source
     Naming me. That source I return to
     When skin is torn, mangled and I possess
     No mending arts. But what is life in armies
     But baths in rusty blades? Father dies.
     Words freeze in memory. Touch bequeaths ashes.
     Silence. A shaky bridge I must walk in pain.
     Father. Source blowing away from my anxious,
     Grasping fingers.

14   There comes time I call my bonny.
Call my bonny back to me. Comes time
when I call pieces of my life. Saying I
Don't know what tomorrow may bring. But knowing
Unused scraps of my soul will moan
To rising suns. I left the army calling
My bonny without bones of your sounds
To heal my weary soul. Yet there comes time
I call my bonny. Bring my bonny back to me.
Visions in my presence are decadent
As rusted wires/wild around rotted wood.
I bring my bonny back. Chicago and the post office
Like hangnails. Everytime I move pain warns me
To stop. Everywhere I go cops shoot Blacks
Over water faucets; Blacks kill Vietnamese
For blood money. Dances in the streets revive
Old djs to spin jams for bold men rising
From fathers nursed on blueberry hills.

15 The sixties,
    I told Black people, it would be all right
    If they changed my name/changed my name.
    Stokely says friends will not know you
    If Black power change your name/change your name.
    I said man, it will be all right
    If it change my name/change my name.
    King says your enemies will pursue you
    If freedom change your name/change your name.
    I said it will be all right
    If it change my name/change my name.
    The sixties,
    I rise screaming from the dead
    Cause I be so glad I change my name.
    The sixties,
    My blood running like it must have
    When Gabriel, Denmark, and Nat realized long ago
    That history cannot be put off.
    The sixties,
    Black people change my name.
    I am touched by moanings in daybreak-talking storms.
    The sixties,
    Malcolm is executed
    King is murdered
    Little Bobby sacrificed
    And Fred Hampton is assassinated.
    I am touched. Fred lying in a box.
    Country Preacher speaking from a nearby record shop
    To the cold wet day.
    The sixties,
    I am touched/really touched.

A warrior lying with red books on his chest.
Panthers marching to push hurtsongs
From tomorrow's heart.
The sixties,
I remember isles of sweet livelihoods, black town.
I change my name in documents by fire.
People melting steel to take their shadows
And spin images from movement.
The sixties,
My people discovering tiers of their lives in flames.
Changing my name.

16 The sixties,
Youth says it can no longer be my friend.
My voice
Leaping with Black choirs.
The sixties,
I salivate/trying to lean with youth.
I slip into the seventies
To the present. Willie says will it be all right
If I change your name/change your name.
I said it will be all right
If you change my name.
He says the present will be a dangerous place
To live if I change your name/change your name
I said it will be all right
If you change my name. I awake
My past running along like Ellington songs.
The seventies,
My youth withering like love songs.
The seventies,
I will be all right/I changed my name. . .

Zimbabwe

(for Freedom Fighters)

Take this
black mother's anguish and wave
breezes of fight
on the hands,
common hands, the true owners of man;
wave fits
of historical necessity, violence cleansing.
Listen
as slave mothers sigh
for children killed to stop blood
from wearing another's name;
listen to their vows
to birth avengers, common hands,
the working integers of order.

Take this black worth
this silent song of black mothers
and throw it out on fields
sprinkle your earth with seeds
those precious fortune peddlers
of tomorrow. Reach past Soweto's screams,
grab the mothers's pain
twisted by knowing
each hour
their blood will flow;

each hour their children will call
for parents to bury them;
grab that pain
and paper your chants with it.

You are
makers straining sunshine from darkness.
You, breakers of the demon's hold
                of the imperialists' strangle
                of colonial grip,
portray the future in gladness
because you are the day torn from a cloud
a wrecking crew of time
summoned to cure Rhodesia's existence.
Earth shakers
you wound the tiger
stick openings in his side
so his roar becomes a death cry
and all hands, common hands,
can clap for your victory
because it is also theirs.

Take this,
our mothers' anguish:
widows of lynchees silently praying defiance
runaways' mothers sobbing in uncertainty.
Take it!
It is yours
because you move.
                Because the day you make
is the day of tomorrow.
Because from your hands
come
the common hands' destiny

I Hear the Shuffle of the People's Feet

i am a name clanging
against circles

i go round
in what's been said and done
the old puts leashes
on my eyes
i go round
in tribal wisdom

men walking from the sea
as if it is dry land
enter my circle
put me in a straight line
from profit to death
i turn from now
back to the past
they fold my future
in their bank accounts

they take me from hands
to memory
i move from knowledge
to obedience
i plant tobacco
i train sugarcane
i yessir masters
i go straight from sunrises
to death
when i remember
i chant shango
i sing ogun
i dance obatala
i hum orishas

i am folded in work
i get up
i obey
i rebel
i runaway
they beat production
from my bones
and track up my mind
with their language

after one generation
i go round in silence
while my children work
without ever knowing tribal hands
they echo my songs
until whips dull their voices

i survive dungeons
by singing songs shaped by brutality:
i sing new necessities
in a strange band
my songs carry
rhythmic cries of my journey
and when i dance
yes, when i dance
i revive tribal possessions
the elders' hands
twist my eyes on right
and let my body go

true believer, the whip
tells my mind
what to dream
i feel the blood of africa
dripping down my back

though my pride rises
in what i do
to destroy the masters' blade
sinning against my skin
true believer, i survive
yes, i survive, i keep going
though they take everything away
i survive america

my name is written
in blood-wrapped days
untold centuries of cruelty
but i survive
come into the union
through a crack
my fist made
i had experienced
breaking freedom holes
by laying underground railroads
by plotting at night
by striking blows

they closed equality's door
before i could enter
they sent me bluesing towns
facing hostility
with open-eyed moans
i get my woman
from the master's bed
but lose her to his kitchen
learn every road
from all my searching
and not one of them end at opportunity
they send me bluesing towns

when I get the vote
terror drives me into fear
the tar, ropes, and evil men
scar my name with blood

they puke their fright and weaknesses
on me
instead of on those who own our bones
though they slaughter
still they cannot stop my efforts
i survive
following rivers to cities
putting my story on brass and winds

i live tyranny down
by swinging with jazz
but the white man's word
places hinges on my sky
from the shadows
i hear plantations talk
the civil war
sets me free from legal whippings
but not from lashes

when booker t prayed conformity
at backseat rites
i could hear lynchees scream
i could hear frightened men cry
i walked with DuBois
at Niagara
they jailed my reputation
in smelly epithets
yet i survive their onslaught
distance between freedom and chains
is measured by steps from backseats
to defiance

i move by going
where there ain't no fields
going where bondage is to production
to the factory's commands
in detroit
chicago
cleveland and milwaukee
away from hot suns
away from boll weevils
away from droughts
to a new world

my music affirms demons
barking resistence in my veins
and i sing ragtime gospels
hi-de-hi-hos hoochie coochies
my girls and temptation walks
in leaving the land
my legacy is transformed
in citified jive sayings

they take me to the work line
but leave my freedom at the station
listening to rails retell the places
i have not arrived at yet
i am still motherless
yet a hip-cat-rhinehart-zoot-suiting
malcolming wolf-waters shoeshine stone
i am a bigger bad trigger greedy
no-name boy prowling chitown
they put ethel in my waters
and she emerges lady day
pestering orchards of my soul
she-goddess of this strangeness
lady instrumentalized voice
tingling new sounds in new times

what the whip and lynchings
didn't get on the land
hard work, high prices, and the hawk
took away on these streets
they send me bluesing towns
"i ain't got nobody/got nobody
just me and my telephone"
i burn from exploitation
i empty my soul on fads
powdery substances Messiahs stand on

i mau-mau stampedes
against racist stalls
bellowing "for your precious love
means more to me
than any love can ever be"
the work songs rise
to become freedom anthems

the Supreme Court hears my lyrics
and its laws change beats
"separate but equal"
becomes "equality for all"
malcolm speaks/speaks so sweet
i hear the shuffle of the peoples' feet
we move in montgomery
we move in little rock
we move
we move at sit-in counters
we move on freedom rides
we move
we move in birmingham
we move on registration drives
we move
malcom speaks/speaks so sweet.

doin the riot/i fall from new bags
with a world fighting back
in viet nam
in angola
in mozambique
in the panther walks
poppa gotta rebellion thing
momma wears a freedom ring
freedom rings
from every alley and hole
brother, come here quick
take this struggle stick
freedom rings
the get black
burning too
take all the streets
do the boogaloo
freedom rings
feel so good
black out loud
dancing in the streets
with the fighting crowd

doin the riot
the burning too
throwing molotov cocktails
making black power new

we move
malcolm speaks/speaks so sweet.
i hear the shuffle of the peoples' feet

Steps to Break the Circle: An Introduction

What happened in the making of Black poetry in the sixties is not different from what happened in the shaping of any other aspect of what we tried to do. There were screamers or, as Eugene Redmond would say, ranters who could not rite, who hastily told us we were beautiful because we were black; that we were revolutionary because we were black; that we were proud because we were black; because we were nationalists; because we stopped eating the pig; because we could shake hands for days; because we greeted in Swahili or Yoruba and made references to Allah instead of Jehovah.

And, similarly, a lot of garbage passed for black poetry. The poets, like the other ranters, with their tongues in somebody's ass, as Ayi Kwei Armah might have put it, were not allergic to bullshit. Much of the ranting was no more than a bunch of slogans with ready sentimental appeal, headed for the marketplace. But where was the poetry? Not that there is anything wrong with slogans. They do serve their purpose. *Portugal out of*

Mozambique, shouted at an anti-imperialist rally in support of liberation movements, is a very concrete, appropriate and moving comment. But after a rally or a demonstration, of what use are the picket signs?

Fortunately, there were those who were moved by Fanon, by Nkrumah, by Malcolm, by Cabral, by Moumie, by Cuba, by Vietnam, by SNCC—remember *Black Power* and *What does a penny buy!* There were those who worked diligently, who were not literary adventurists, opportunists or plain simple-ass whores; those who will continue to produce a poetry steeped in reality; those who propose to "take steps to break the circle" of deathbound confusion and limpminded posturing. Sterling Plumpp is one of those.

Steps to Break the Circle is not an entertaining poem, no. The memory and the vision of this poem take us back to the mid-sixties in North America; but really, in its power, to any time as any place where

The Black Man drags his chain
His steel tail
And his tales ring
With the muddy sound of pain

So *Steps to Break the Circle* begins, and *deals*, with the sixties. There is this young brother who leaves Mississippi confused, searching for his blackness, his mystical identity, his hocuspocus belief that essentially after he has found his blackness his problems will be solved. But the Staple Singers, when they were still a straightup gospel troupe, had already posed this question in *Will the Circle be Unbroken*, which is a kind of petty bourgeois luxury, which had already been posed by the literati of the 'Harlem Renaissance' twenties and the Negritude evolues of the thirties in Europe, and earlier, at the turn of the century, by DuBois' double consciousness trap of the talented tenth, much, much more slippery than the pus from a gum with an absess or the blood from a tricky menstrual flow. The Staple Singers Sang:

I was standin by my window
On a cold and cloudy day
When I saw the hearse
Come arollin . . . ooh . . .
To take my mother away
Will the circle be unbroken

Sterling Plumpp's poem takes off from that.

I was standing on a corner
On that cold, cold rainy day
When they blew Malcolm away.
Will the circle be unbroken
Bye and bye, yall, bye and bye . . .

Outside of the authentic black musician, Langston Hughes, Zora Neale Hurston, James Weldon Johnson, Leon Damas, Martin Carter, Ama Ata Aidoo, Ho, Mao, Guillen, p'Bitek, Achebe, Sterling Brown, Julia Fields, Henry Dumas, Ayi Kwei Armah, Margaret Walker, Alston Anderson, Ellison, in spite of himself, occasionally Baldwin, Tolson, Mphahlele, Hayden and Peter Abrahams when he is inspired by forces beyond his control, it is difficult to find writers in the embat-

tled zone of literate expression in a European
language who endow it with the weight and
the depth of the rhythms of our life. Among
the 'younger' writers Sterling Plumpp certainly does it past any argument:

Undertaker he took Brother King
Laid him out in a shroud
As the troubled cloud
Gave birth to my agony,
Now will the circle be unbroken

Brother Malcolm and King have been wasted,
so this young blood leaves 'warm Mississippi
for cold Chi'!

And I wanders on, on blacktop hunches
Trying to make a straight bound train
A train to train all my brothers
Travel with all the sisters
And trample, trample my enemy, . . .

But the city is a strange place. Sterling
Plumpp knows that with a brutal clarity and
he shows it to be that way with admirable
skill, pushing the word to song past the hasty
loudness of the ranters Fanon warned us
against. On the train the young man meets
an older sister, Caldonia's mama—remember
Caldonia of Louis Jourdan fame? Caldonia's
mama does not go to Chicago, no, "I just
visits, just visits chi," because she knows that

My old bones got permanent homes
Down deep deep in Mississippi . . .

where

Our peoples pulls up the rascal weeds
And picks only the good crops

But in the cold windy city they

Dances for the big big harvests
And reaps nothing but dry grass. . . .
The lights maybes lighter
But I knows the whites is whiter
And the darks ain't no darker

Caldonia's mama, Reverend, the ubiquitous
preacherman, and the old, old man,
grandpa, all try to advise this young brother
not to go to cold, windy Chicago where he is
convinced that "opportunity hides under/con-
crete like sweet taters." In the city he runs
into Caldonia who has been whipped even
out of her personal identity:

Naw, baby, I ain't no Caldonia.
I be more like the pneumonia,
Cold cold city sucks my tiddies. . . .
I can't even get a bowl of chili
And I ain't see no collards
Let alone some green ones.
Baby, in this cold cold city
You lucky if you gets soup bones.

And she advises him to leave this city where
black folks "ain't nothing but baby chickens."
But he refuses to leave until it is much too
late.

There is nothing like the blind, mystical belief in the virtues of the rural South here, or
that mystifying pastoral nonsense the Euro-
peans trapped us into. The sun rises in the
east and sets in the west anywhere on this
planet. And all skies are blue, whether you
are in Angola Louisiana, or Angola, southern
Africa. After all, the rural South is part of

North America, and was not designed, or ordered, for our comfort, benefit or interest. So when the young blood wants to leave the city after his personal disillusionment, all the people who had initially advised him not to leave Mississippi now advise him to stay in Chicago. He is still hardheaded but when he gets back to Mississippi to "drink your change,"

Nigger, what you seen
Wasn't no dust of change rising.
It was the dust of sameness settling.

Well, will the circle be broken? Certainly not by running between Mississippi and Chicago, or whatever other areas of hideous European design—whether your flight is by train or plane. It will not be broken by equally hideous escapist fantasy because!

How can the circle be broken
Young man, when you is riding
Riding in the easy chair of the circle?

And now the young man ain't so young no more, though he, at this point, seems to still believe that the fervor of black nationalism is the answer, as if Senghor, or Banda, or Houphouet-Boigny, or Selassie, are not African. Although:

Black folks is seeing themselves
Pretty and big time.
There ain't no more Negroes
Ain't no more straightening combs,
Ain't no more looking like white folks.
They is Africans

The circle remains unbroken; in spite of all the dashikis, all the huge, immaculate afros, all the fists up in the air proclaiming our pride in blackness. To the casualty list add Nigeria of the late sixties, add Uganda, add Nkrumah, add Cabral, add Rap, add Tiro, add Robben Island, add the seven principles, and what do you come up with?

Until we develop to a level of social consciousness that forces us to be systematic and coldly programmatic, we are playing a very perverse game, a kind of self-righteous masturbation more hideous than whoring.

Sterling Plumpp, very much like Ayi Kwei Armah—as witness the Naana segments of *Fragments*—evidently has a lot of respect for collected and collective wisdom and the way that that wisdom is systematically ordered in terms of idiom, in terms of syntax, in terms of image, in terms of tone and depth of feeling and pattern of thinking, in terms of nuance—nothing like what the commercial publisher would mean by those self-same terms with dollar green eyes glued on the package at the marketplace. Check out the authenticity of each character's diction, coming from the specific corner of North America they wake up in and are most responsive to.

Keorapetse Kgositsile

New Orleans, April, 1974.

Steps to Break the Circle

I was standing on a corner
On that cold, cold rainy day
When they blew Malcolm away.
Will the circle be unbroken
Bye and bye, yall, bye and bye . . .

The Black Man's days are epic chains
Superbad links wandering in cisterns
Dry and narrow with the unending
Echoes just jazzing nights
Riffing right through wooden walls.
These trips I takes is waking breaths
Life cycles my fathers left me pedaling.
My Mississippi manning is a message
Kilos of soul cider sipped by the music
Of a song sailed over sage oceans . . .
I wears the rapping ring of seasons
Ebony circles of blues with the road
Long and my tired strides short.
Mocking birds' mimics are mentors
I hears my soul striding down gravel
Years and the dust is dancing . . .

Undertaker he took Brother King
Laid him out in a shroud
As the troubled cloud
Gave birth to my agony,
Now will the circle be unbroken
Bye and bye, yall, bye and bye . . .

The Black Man's days are epics changing
Bigfeet to break the circle
Break the breast of beaded crises
Ships stinking with Black flesh
Cottonfields colorful with open locks
Muddy roads with stubborn mules tugging

Rivers coughing up African bodies
Fathers never seeing their chilluns mature
Chilluns never knowing their fathers,
Steps to break the circle, I takes
When I lets the leaves become
Victims of crazy winds
And I wanders on, on blacktop hunches
Trying to make a straight bound train
A train to train all my brothers
Travel with all the sisters
And trample, trample my enemy,
This train this train this train
I rides is a hundred cars long. . . .

"Young man, chance you meet my chile,
Call her Caldonia, old Caldonia. . . .
My Caldonia is a long tall, gal.
My Caldonia is a long tall, gal.
You'll know my Caldonia Caldonia
She is a real life chile;
Her laugh is loud, her face pretty.
My Caldonia got a brand new man,
Left her other one shooting craps
Down on the old old levee.
If you should see my Caldonia
Tell her, her momma is well
And is visiting cold chi.
I haven't seen my chile in years
And my legs is too too tired
To walk, walk all over chi."

"Ma'am, if I should see your Caldonia,
If I meets your Caldonia,
I'll tell her, her momma was in chi.
But, ma'am why dos an old old woman
Leave warm Mississippi for cold chi?"

"Young man, I don't go to chi,
I just visits, just visits chi.
My old bones got permanent homes
Down deep deep in Mississippi . . .
Son, I tells you, you is running
Running from the rich rich soil

Where your folks soul is planted
Way down deep in Mississippi's belly.
You should be wing flappin' it South
Instead rocking on the rails of cold chi,
Cause in Mississippi, in Mississippi,
Our peoples pulls up the rascal weeds
And picks only the good crops.
But in cold cold windy city they dances
Dances for the big big harvests
And reaps nothing but dry grass.
There is daybreak in the South
And all you young youngarns
Should stay underkivver in black soil
Cause soon you gonna rise, rise
Up high in the heavens to glory.
Listen, I sees the sun raising his head
Over the hilltops, eavesdropping
On the sweet sweet morning dew."

"But, Ma'am, I gotta, gotta go,
Just gotta go to the windy city,
I told my momma I would go
I told my baby I would go
Where the lights is lighter"

"Son, I know you gon do
What you gon do
But listen about the windy city,
The cold cold windy city.
The lights maybes lighter
But I knows the whites is whiter
And the darks ain't no darker"

"Your people don't live in the windy city,
They lives in the rotten rotten
Tiddy of that old old windy city.
Son, I tells you we black folks
Is caught, caught in the fist . . ."
Now will the circle be unbroken
Bye and bye, yall, bye and bye . . .

The Black Man's days are epic changes
The pocket money of hip new moons
Seasons where tides two steps
Against blind shores.
You hear the light pennies jingle
In a Black Man's strides.
No matter how a Black Man steps
It is for better stairs
Because the wild fires
Are flipping coins for his ass.

"Young man, do you know the Lord?
Do you know? Do you know what
You are living for?
I see see you is riding
Young man, but where is you going?"

"Reverend, my feet have holes
From the hard red clay
And I is heading for the cold city.
I ain't never had nothing
But a big old opened door,
Troubles on my mind and
Nobody to tell me where to go.
I'm going to chi
Even if I gits there on my knees."

"Turn round, turn round.
You is leaving the sun.
I knows that peoples tell you in chi
Lights is lighter
But there ain't no sun."

"But I gotta go to the windy city
And make my dreams come true.
I must live on big streets
Dance to big bands
And get rich from living. . . ."
Will the circle be unbroken
Bye and bye, yall, bye and bye . . .

"Young man, young man,
You looks like worries on your mind.
Be careful, boy, and find out
Who you is. I knows evahbody
On this train is chi bound
But they is also bound
In the noose of the circle.
They going from town to town
And wherever they goes
They never have a place to stay.
Son, you youngarns talks bout
Them rock and roll shoes.
Put them on your foots
And rock against the circle
Roll steps to break the bad
Of the barrelling circle.
But yalls going the wrong way,
Go back! Go back to Mississippi
Where changes is kicking up
His heels, thumping up dust,
I sees it rising like brown clouds."

"Look, grandpa, old old man,
I knows what I is doing.
I is going to the city
Where opportunity hides under
Concrete like sweet taters.
I knows I can dig what
I digs up from the ground.
I ain't, ain't going back
Down to mister Mississippi."
Will the circle be unbroken
Bye and bye, yall, bye and bye . . .

The Black Man's days are epic chores
Roars of unheeded deeds
Columns of soldiers to kill.
The Black Man drags his chain
His steel tail
And his tales ring
With the muddy sound of pain.

"Hey, man, is you going to chi,
Going to that big fine city.
Chi ain't sad as miss Mississippi
With her bitch hurt trapping us."

"Yea, baby, I'm on my way to chi,
Mississippi's ground will never
Hold my foots at sundown.
I'm on my way, I'm on my way
And I can't turn around,
I'm on my way to the windy city"
Now will the circle be unbroken
Bye and bye, yall, bye and bye. . . .

The Black Man's days are epics chasing
Windy shuffles running for thrills
The blue bird of pain chirping loud
Calling on buried hours to rise.
The Black Man does not take his steps.
They takes him along, alone . . .
The sound of his steps is a weak
Awakening, a wondering where nasty
Noises will end and the bad bad music
Of bold dances make the scene.
To take your steps you must prep
Must prep your mind then preach
Preach pacing rhythms to your toes.
The Black Man must sic the sickle
On the circle before he breaks
The cells of his anemia . . .

"Hey! You is Caldonia Caldonia,
I meets your momma on the train,
She say she's in cold cold chi."

"Naw, baby, I ain't no Caldonia.
I be more like the pneumonia,
Cold cold city sucks my tiddies.
You didn't meet my momma, honey.
It was your own momma you met
Telling you that if you left
The soft soft tiddies of the south
Nothing would be left for your mouth."

"But, you is Caldonia Caldonia,
Cause you laugh is loud, your face
Was pretty pretty and you answers
When I calls you Caldonia Caldonia.
I knows you is Caldonia Caldonia.
I smells chitlins and collards greens
Fussing up a storm on your breath."

"Honey, your mind is tricking you.
I can't even get a bowl of chili
And I ain't see no collards
Let alone some green ones.
Baby, in this cold cold city
You lucky if you gets soup bones.
Hogs and greens don't grow here
In this old old windy city
And they cost bout as much
As T-bone steaks and taters.
Honey, you leave this city
Cause Black folks in it
Ain't nothing but baby chickens."

"I can't, I can't leave this city,
I comes to find myself
I comes to get a start in life."

"Baby, you gotta start
Had better start running
Running back to Mississippi."
Will the circle be unbroken
Bye and bye, yall, bye and bye . . .

The Black Man's days are epic clues
The blues clung to the blue blue sky
And black skillets dry and empty
Mosaic seconds trying to second
The motion of age old pictures.
The Black Man must touch kettles of blood
Teach the tongue of torches
Speak to brews of bursting
And whisper in eyes of blasting
Before he takes his steps . . .

"I wants a job, I can break up . . .
I can break the bold pavement.
I comes from mister Mississippi
And I needs a job in cold chi."

"We don't need nobody today.
Leave your name and come back
Tomorrow we may need black backs."

"I gots to git work to come back
Cause my belly is slack as a sack
My clothes too thin for this wind
In this old and cold cold city.
I needs to make some money,
I needs a part of my fortune."

"We can't help you
With work and money.
Go to a fortune teller
He'll tell your fortune
Cause in this mean windy city
Fortunes just blow away . . ."
Now will the circle be unbroken
Bye and bye, yall, bye and bye . . .

The Black Man's days are epic claims
Stakes in the snagga teeth of time
Gold rushes for diamond rights
Clogged in tipsy wheel of change.
I meditates hard when I takes
My Black Man's steps, steps
That have taken me down sound years . . .

"Young man, young man, you ain't,
Ain't leaving windy city is you?
I told you not to leave when
You was leaving, but stay now.
It wont be a cold cold city long."

"I is leaving this cold city
Cause all I found was the wind
And much too much sin sin . . .
Even your Caldonia Caldonia
Say she wasn't Caldonia when I
Calls her your Caldonia Caldonia.
Nobody wants to be what they is
And everybody ain't nobody . . .
I shoulda listened and seen
Changes jumping up and down
Like you told me to do.
Now I knows the south is,
Is changing change and I gon
Go back and change some, too."

"Young man, young man, things
Was changing but that is over.
Now they gitting ready to stop,
Down deep in the sweating south.
But up here in this cold city
I feels the heat of closeness,
I knows change gon boil over.
You stay in windy winter city."
Will the circle be unbroken
Bye and bye, yall, bye and bye . . .

The Black Man's days are epic chants
Soul stockings rung on rungs
Tears tipping up laughing ladders
The holy hands of juju holding
Onto the handles of shouting.
The Black Man grinds his days
Into wisdom sausages
Links of sermons walking walking . . .

"Young man, young man, didn't you
Find?—didn't you find yourself?
Young men should be in the cold
Old windy windy and chi city
when the hot combs of change
Come and begins to curl wrongs.
Son, the Lord wants you
Wants you to stay in cold chi."

"But Reverend, I hears voices
Voices down in Dixie calling
Calling softly in my ears . . .
They says changes is strutting
With signs falling down
Like the mighty walls of Jericho.
Black and white is walking
Hand in hand.
Black eyes is sprung open
Like dynamite blown caves."

"Son, your changes will dry up
By the time you reach Mississippi.
All you gon find is the dry dusty
The dust of uncultivated dreams.
Stay here in this windy city
The winds gon let you win. . . ."

"But Reverend, why dos you tell
Me to stay, stay here, when
You goes from place to place?
I is a young man and can go
More easily than you can.
Why don't you stay and live?"

"Son, old men ain't looking,
They is already found, found life
By living it daily for many years.
I ain't never leave Mississippi
And I is in the windy windy city
Even fore I gits on the train.
Son, I knows who I is
And I is just here living."
Now will the circle be unbroken
Bye and bye, yall, bye and bye . . .

The Black Man's days are epic charges
Account of ships through yearly deaths
Debts of cowardice shooting dice
The menu of running and crying
Accusations of anguish ringing
The big bells of ancient troubles.

"Old man, old man, why dos—
Why dos you carry a rocking chair?
I met you going to windy city
Now I meets you with a easy chair.
Why dos a old old man travel?"

"Son, I don't ever travel,
I just bes, just bes everywhere.
You don't see traveling.
What you see is your own life
Roaming in this wide world.
My chair is for to witness and ride
Witness the rocking changes
And ride the easy breezes of knowing.
Son, you is going the way
The circle wants you to go.
Stop! And takes steps. . . ."
Will the circle be unbroken
Bye and bye, yall, bye and bye . . .

The Black Man's days are epic chambers
Rooms at the top of passion
Upper layers of sagging hot clouds
Closet music suffocating from drought
Old old maids skipping alone
Down dusk dark and dusty roads
Big shot cells of death waiting . . .

"Hey, bro, is you going,
Going down to the changing south?
I is, I feels the sun
All shining in my soul."

"Yeah, baby, I is going down,
Down in the south
And sit with the magic sun."

"Oh, you, the dude, I sees when
I is on my way, on my way
Up to that windy city.

But, bro, is you got a home
A home way down yonder
In the rock of Mississippi
Where you sees the black soil?"

"Bro, no need worry bout homes.
We all gots homes deep down
Down in the soul of the south:
We gots all those collard greens
Butter beans peas and okra
We gots long rows of cotton
And fields of tall corn
We gots the promised land
Way down, way down in the south."

"Yeah, man, but I leaves the south
And meets you leaving too.
I also meets Caldonia' momma,
A preacher man and an old old man
Leaving the south . . .
How comes everybody leaves
Mississippi if it the promised land?"
Will the circle be unbroken
Bye and bye, yall, bye and bye . . .

The Black Man's days are epic churns
Soul clabber of hope fluttering
His happy wings
The turning timbre of toils
Big wheels of wicked man hours
Rolling from Africa all
Through the Wide Diaspora.
The Black Man must muse his muscles
To reel the turning turning wheel
He must scythe the circle
To psyche in his black cycles.
I walks the spare ribs of whips
Robbing my wounds of their pain
I takes my teaching steps
When I takes hold of my mind . . .

"Mister Mississippi, Mississippi
I is come back to drink your change,
I is come back to flow with you
I is come back to your warm arms."

"Nigger, you shoulda stayed up
Up in that old cold city
Where gold is beneath the concrete.
You shoulda stayed up where
Tall tall buildings just glow
With the bright lights of life.
Nigger, you shoulda stayed
Stayed in the windy city."

"I comes back cause Caldonia's momma
Told me to stay when I was leaving.
The preacher man told me to stay
When I was leaving and that
Old old man told me the same thing.
I didn't find no waiting gold
And couldn't see no tall
Tall buildings for the dirt.
I comes back home to Mississippi
Cause I sees all them changes
Rising up like dust storms."

"Nigger, what you seen
Wasn't no dust of changes rising.
It was the dust of sameness settling.
Nigger, you ain't never gon change
Until you change your steps.
You steps round into circles
And you ain't going nowhere."

"I can't stand still when yellow jackets
Is all over my naked back biting
And talking their tight fitting shit.
I gotta touch this Mississippi soil
And feel my warm home way down
Deep in Mississippi's bones . . ."

"Nigger, circle steppers ain't got
Aint got no home, nowheres.
You gotta take steps
To make your home . . ."
Now will the circle be unbroken
Bye and bye, yall, bye and bye . . .

The Black Man's days are epic chapels
Sistine fumes of cinnamon incense
Carrying the holy coughdrops
The a cappella chants of voodoo love
Calls coming from blacker black cherries
Treed by the moist morning dew
Big temples of temptations
Where lovely bells hang on hinges.

"Momma, oh Momma!
I done come home to Mississippi
And missed them changes rising.
I left that old cold city
Where the storm clouds of troubles
Hung like a mighty big quilt
That blots out all daylight.
Momma, I can't find no home
No matter where I goes.
Me and that old long train
Is the best of best friends.
The only road I knows
Is the railroad, it goes
All the way from Mississippi
Up to the windy city's door"

"Son, you shoulda stayed up in
In that there windy windy city
Cause what you thought
Was quilted clouds of troubles,
Wasn't nothing but darkness
Fore the morning sun rises . . .
Them chilluns up North
Is dancing steps I members
My great great grandparents did.
They is reaching out to grab
Hold of our fatherland images.
Nights, I can't sleep for the tom-tom

Of their proud feet prancing
Like fine thoroughbreds.
Them young people is change,
With they hair like God made it,
Son, you shoulda stayed North . . ."

"Momma! I'm going back
Back to that sweet old city
Even if all she offers me
Is her big rotten tiddies.
I ain't gon let Mississippi's dust
Settle down on my head.
I'm going to the windy city . . ."

"Naw, son! You shoulda stayed
Up in that cold cold city,
Not go back there.
Now stay where you is at."

"This is where I was
Cause I'm gon fly back
To that mean mean city
Like the flight of a coletrane . . ."
Will the circle be unbroken
Bye and bye, yall, bye and bye . . .

My Black Man's days are epic cold cuts
Minced meat of black meanings
Lying on platters of prison
Titanic cucumbers in vinegar
Coffers filled to the very brim
Whole wheat bread of badness
Sandwiched round a leaning me.
I must munch my moans
Fore I kindles the candles of my moves.
The steps I takes are
In a whirling whirling groove
And I goes round and round . . .

"Young man, young man, you
Ain't young young no more.
Already I sees them years
Is turning your hair gray
Like night into daybreak.
Go back, back to Mississippi.
I done seen you twice on trains
And now you is flying, flying
Up to that old cold city."

"I wants to find my home
Find my home in the many
Many mansions of the city.
I got a home
You got a home
All God's chilluns got homes
In that windy windy city."

"Son. Will the circle be broken,
Will the circle be broken
Bye and bye when you
Puts your steps right down
And stand on your own land?"

"When I gets to my city
I'm gonna put on a long robe
And sing sing to the broken circle.
I'm gonna make my steps
Stop the bold circle . . ."

"How can the circle be broken,
Young man, when you is riding
Riding in the easy chair of the circle?
Young man you gotta wayfare
In the wilderness of your land
To break the circle. Go back
Back down to Mississippi
And break rich new grounds . . ."
Now will the circle be unbroken
Bye and bye, yall, bye and bye . . .

My Black Man's days are epic cards
Tricky deals of bad hands
Deuces coming when aces
Are needed to beat bills
Spotted decks of sorrows stretching
From Benin's face to Birmingham's walls.

"Son, didn't you find?
Didn't you find. . . ?
You leaving your Canaan, son,
And going to Sodom-Gomorrah.
Your promised land is under your foots.
You is leaving home.
Who's gonna cook your bread?
Who's gonna clean your clothes?
Who's gonna make your beds?
Who's gonna know your name?
Who's gonna keep you well?
Who's gonna make you happy?
Young man, young man,
You still young enough
To turn back, go back
Way down, oh deep down
In Mississippi, mister Mississippi."

"But, Reverend, I gots to go
Mississippi ain't no home
And I don't want to die
Of heart trouble like my poppa did."

"Young man, young man, we
All dies of hard trouble.
Son, you is in big troubles
Trapped in the thorns of the circle
You is like Daniel in the lion's den
Waiting in the whirling circle.
Son, you gotta be delivered
Delivered from the devious circle.
But didn't my Lord deliver Daniel
Didn't my God deliver Daniel
Deliver old Daniel from the lion's den.
And didn't my God deliver Jonas
Didn't my God deliver Jonas
Deliver old Jonas from the belly of the whale?

And didn't my God deliver King
Didn't my God deliver King
Deliver old King from a Birmingham jail?
Son, my God can deliver!
My God can deliver
Deliver you from the cross of the circle.
But before you is delivered
You gotta desire deliverance
You gotta take saving steps
Steps to break the bucking and bragging circle."

"But, Reverend, I ain't got
No god to break my circle.
I is looking, looking for my god.
That's why I is always going
From places to places.
I is searching . . ."

"Young man, young man, every
Man got a god cause god
Ain't nothing but the cord
Tying him to his own life.
You is cutting the string
By running from Mississippi.
You is you own savior
When you uses your own life
As clippers to shape steps
Steps to break the circle you in."
Will the circle be unbroken
Bye and bye, yall, bye and bye . . .

My Black Man's days are epic charms
Nommo jingles bopping in blue waters
Crescent balls set in the nappy head
Of a bad-assed pyramid
Wooing touches of slender
Sunflowers flowing naked in the sun.

"Old man, old man, where
Is your rocking chair?
Why is you flying when you
Ain't got no need to hurry?"

"Son, I ain't flying,
But I is on this plane.
And I don't need no rocking chair
When I can sit here and
Rock and cheer
Rock on the rock of my life
And cheer the days I lived,
I got a home in my life.
But, son, why is you leaving
Your home in your life
Way down, deep down south
And flying to windy windy city?"

"I is going cause that's
Where changes is dancing.
Black folks is seeing themselves
Pretty and big time.
There ain't no more Negroes
Ain't no more straightening combs,
Ain't no more looking like white folks.
They is Africans
And if white folks don't like it,
It's too bad, too bad
Cause they got guns and matches
And is ready to fight back."

"Son, you is on the couch
The tricky couch of the circle
And you thinks change is there
When all the changes is in you,
You gotta change your steps . . ."
Now will the circle be unbroken
Bye and bye, yall, bye and bye . . .

My Black Man's days are epic curtains
Drawn shades of my light moments
Pyramidal drapes of red, green and black
Shaking their round asses to the beat
Of a tom-tom and conked conga
Falling dreams sliding down
To ponderous claps of wonder.

"I'm a go-go-go-go-rilla,
I'm the hope of the new nation.
You can see my da-da-da-da-shiki
And my big ivoryebony carved tiki.
Man! I'm a go-go-go-go-go-rilla . . .
You goin' to the renamed land, bro?
You goin' to our thang?
Bro, I is changed black.
My head is soot natural
My language grapes from the grapevine.
I can tell you how to get black."

"I is trying to be me, bro.
I is ready for blackness.
I wanna be black me.
I wanna be black me."

"Bro, all you gotta do
Is put your bad, your bad
Nigger spirit in the air
Spread out the musty funk
Breathe the holy halitosis
Spit out the wretched words
Vomit your undid deeds
Bro, shit out the nasty waste
Piss the stingy water
Put your bad, your bad
Nigger spirit in the air
And leave that hip muthafucka
Doin' the Penguin out there"
Will the circle be unbroken
Bye and bye, yall, bye and bye . . .

My Black Man's days are epic combs
Tattered teeth of time biting
Into the raw pork chops of running
Brushes with the clawed law
Curls in the head of wanting
Honey on the bare tongue of
The panting years . . .

"Mister windy city, windy city,
I is come here to you.
I hears that Blackness is here,
I is come back to you."

"Young man, my whole west side
Is burned black and blue.
All that's left is land,
Now you can build on me.
Blackness is a song of cleansing
Burning out the filth.
White folks need Blackness
To stay well, they need fire
But they is sleep now.
I'm an old windy windy city.
Have seen millions come
And millions going away
Seeking the reins of Truth . . .
Son, the Truth is the nods
Your heart gives your life.
You don't have to seek it
Yet you must not run away
From currents of life . . ."

"Caldonia, Caldonia, I is ready,
Ready to stop the circle.
I feels my power beating songs
In my steaming soul
And I takes my big steps.
This time I ain't
Ain't gon take no train
Ain't gon take no plane
Ain't gon take no car.
I is walking, taking my own steps. . . ."

My Black Man's days are epic candles
Waxed sticks of roaming flares
Lit by the lightning's bright smiles.
I holds my searching light
Gripped in the hands of my heart
As I shango down the freedom road.

My feetsounds is thunder blows
I shango I shango shango shango
Shango down the freedom road . . .

The Mojo Hands Call/I Must Go

in the night of wakes
i am an old dream
listening to death
i cannot let go
this sticky wheel
this grinding continuation
this iron demand turning & turning
memory pops a whip in my ear
in this space
where my tongue shakes in chills
because my words are frozen
by apathy

i can see yesterday
on the platter of thieves
the old man impaled on the fork
is my father bowing
at the altar of greed
across these alleys tyranny
drugs my hands with fear
crucifies my desire with a knife
here
sitting on the back porch of change
looking out on this city
this brutal mercenary design
crushing even the blood from babies
i can see my history splurged
in marrows of people
who stand weighted past centuries
of unanswered dreams
i can see them clearly now
across alleys of fog
puked up by the machine of illusions

the day they seek
drips with blood from their mothers
they have sealed their ears from the word
the ancestral word/holy root-word
and they wander aimlessly
driven by competitive needles
that have them hooked on consumption
so they suck up their own vomit

the displaced priest there
passionate in his need for reality
with the saturday night special
aimed at the old woman's head
that boy
is curse of this city
that voodoo priest in other click-songs
plagues soil men
for that boy bleeding with terror
could be blasting away
his midwife

the city
this dreadful hole in creation
this colossal pill of stone
i sit in this technological chasm
barricaded from earth
trapped on a bier
where footprints cannot grow
i am one of these children
exiled so low in confusion
that i cannot hear nobody pray
down here
across these treacherous alleys
sometimes words beat saturday night specials to souls
& attica converts stick-up injustice
& panthers stalk lawlessness of the law
& black hands pull ripe images from damnation
& these exiled children of concrete

put righteous flames to oppressive filth

i am bound to this city
hog-tied to this rock seat of disease
this blinding wheel
i cannot let go
so i sit
estranged even from my shadow
in this quarry deep pit
wishing & hoping
hoping & wishing
that somewhere beyond this electric darkness
stars smile from black loaves of night
that somewhere birds prosecute skies with song
& the earth winds & winds
like happy memories
but here
across these windless alleys
the abortion wagons jam traffic
in rush hours of awakening
& the fallen/
brown leaves of my parents
these desperate children
learn they have roots
only to try & define them

i cannot let go
stupidity crowns my head
i am a child/wretched in nerves of day
my view from this city
clicks with deception of mirages
i cannot put my time in reverse
therefore i stare at shattered glass
firing at my eyes

respect walls painted to remove walls
from among us yesterday
have collapsed

i left my heart on the passage of time

that lead shot into fred
is my manhood quashed by inability
those gaping holes in george
are mirrors spelling my courage
the rape & disgrace of joann
was commanded by my default

my fear bone connects to my coward bone
my maybe bone connects to my tomorrow bone

this intensity
this ice-pick explosive
this negligent hurt
riots in my eyes
i cannot let go the wheel
this damned city
i am a child of lost roots
the mojo hand whispers over the universe
tracking the word for my soul
the mojo hand calls hoochie coochie
tracking the word for my soul

i left my life planted in the land
i fled it

came to this celestial wound
this city
this urban gangrene spreading

i came here
so now i sit
across alleys of betrayal

my family screwed in the westside
they notch decades on bones
they share whatever work overlooks
they wait
they share

nothing from these calloused bricks
can cheer their hours

except memories of the land
where juices flushed laughter green
where shadows were kin to bodies
where footprints told stories
where night roared with life
where the spirits drank air

they fled too

came to this wound
they wait
& they share

i pry beneath
these drought-mean alleys
across
          piercing agonies
i search in crevices
of
dust

yet this concrete antenna
this city
draws all the pain into its jaws
then spits it out on channel raw nerves
this city knows no solace
it reeks with hardness of doubt
it sucks blood
& spits out naked skeletons
this city standing on voice of the lake
has no pillows
i sit
across alleys of fire
the children play the dozens
on their veins with needle marks
signify on their spirits

with mainlined overdoses
the boys
my brothers
put on gods of fad
while mocking their fathers's beliefs
the girls
my sisters
let shame penetrate them for pennies
stand on auction corners
waiting for bids to wipe out motherhood
i bless them
with my helplessness
the welfare babies cry
from c. h. a. stalls
they shiver from social sharks
working to devour their pride
they gang in knots
then forget who to bang on
they ride the end passage
many jump overboard
to stationary waves of concrete
the old
my forebears
voice-roots of my nation
they are dug up from respect
& left to dry rot in isolated high rises
they know no greeting
except the snatched purse
or strong-armed robbery
or murder in solitude
or the cold indifference of rushing youth
they fade into graves
while the jade of their lives
are left to swine & flies

my past marks time
on arrogant marble
this city
this weird monstrosity
opaque to goodness

my past hugs these hostile blobs

i sit here
desiring my roots black in soil
but i cannot cannot put my history in reverse
i came here
i came here from roots
in night treks from mississippi
where lawless ropes kill bodies
but whose death peddlings
are mild
compared to murder by this city
(you never exist as a man here)
murder is of the soul/spirit
these evil stones
let no man escape their crunching hands

in death on the land
spirits rock new souls home
lost bodies resurrect in nature
as thunder strikes his bass
as lightning chants soprano vigilance
as clouds clench black fists
& as rains wish down cleanliness
but in this city
this unknowing city
life is ground into particles
spirits are banned
& death is a thud
which nobody notices
i sit
hoping hoochie coochie calls
will bring back the words
the root-words

i left my heart on the passage of time

i fled the word
i came here
to this city
this asphalt-souled mummy
where my commitment hides
behind accomodative curtains
& i hold the strings

here at this junction
even my face testifies against me
because i have no words

only a voice imprisoned in stone

i left my words
dashed away from their stems
left them scattered in winds
so i sit condemned to tread sharp rocks
i cannot let go the wheel
this city
this nightmare slag of emptiness
this ugly detriment
i cannot let go
i came here
& i cannot put my time in reverse

across these pleated bricks
my people
held their words
in cotton fields
on backseats
at baptisms
in church choirs
over hot stoves
at celebrative funerals
in chains
on flights
at births
in hiding places

they held their words
despite lawless ropes
despite downcast eyes
despite the burn of poverty
they held their words
the mojo hand
swung through them like a pendulum
dressed their spirits in welcoming
it swung through them

the mojo hand
roams the whole universe
trying to find a word for my soul
i am modern
rootless
a bastard child of cancer
son of this putrid city
where passion in another day echoes
i hold this wheel
i cannot let go
i fled my word
left my heart on the passage of time

my ears retreat from tunnels of souls
drilling in coveys of voodoo rites
their chains snapping
their names returning
their words boiling
their sounds beckoning beckoning
my ears retreat
because i fled my place
i came here
pain drowns my eyes
my hands shiver in desperation
i want to know space again
but i am bound here
i cannot let go
because i turned my back on the word

i cannot let go
this wheel
this whirling prosecutor
but i hope
i still can flow back to roots
i hope
because the mojo hand promised
it does not lie
i hope
i still can bear fruits
i can get my heart back
i can get my words back
i hope
i shall be unbound/released
to claim my heart from the passage of time
i hope
i can be timeless again
bleeding in the belly of slavery

if i had my heart
i could march across these sounds
& clip ghetto fears
& fall with blood of these children
(i could go down repeatedly)
without the certainty of death
if i had my heart from the passage of time
but i am here
i came here
i fled my roots
i came to this sentencing
without words/holy root-words
i left them passing on time

i drive my tongue
across stench isles
searching for a voice in exasperation
i drive my tongue
& choirs commence
behind smiles

& slaves peddle words in their throats
selling voices along deltas of tears
the voices dance & say come inside islands
come inside skins of your time
i let go
the wheel disappears
rains shake dance in pistons of hope
this welded city loosens its grip
i let go
rising from a cold stone pad
seeing waters entrench these alleys
with their liquid quiet coolness
here in this crumbling hostel
the road appears
the long long road with words
growing on its head
the timeless road waits
i cannot put my time in reverse
but if i walk this road
this gospel peopled road
i shall catch my heart on the passage of time

the mojo hand calls
his hoochie coochie knits music on winds
(i know)
here i am the re-incarnate vow
the desire to be winged in acts
the soul on the cob of self-helping hands
i know there is day
above these ego-cramped skylines
i know
that the road timeless in dark wisdom
that road jewelled with dreams
that tomorrow-drum resonating worlds
that road is my will
if i take hold my soul
& walk from this backside of despair

voodoo wipes my eyes
because the mojo hand works
his hoochie coochie
swings in veins of the moment
i must accept this devil meal
this rip-gut odor boundless
on these children
my brothers
these concrete orphans
i must accept their stench
unbutton shackles
from their facial sties
i must wash my hands in their needs

i must walk this road
i must go
hoochie coochie is calling
he says the mojo hands whisper
the holy mojo hands work
i must walk this road
i must go
i must act
(from this coop of fright)
an eastern sun sips my shadow
laughter of blue skies
cuts through my smoke & fog
i rise from i can
to the doing of it
i move into need
i must walk this road
i must go
i feel this horrible struggle
letting go its pulses
i move farther into need
hearing what my hands
are saying in dance
i am farther in
i am the slayer

i am the maker
the mojo hands
toss me words
their hoochie coochies
initial my soul with roots
come my people,
the mojo hands call/
let us walk this road

Sterling D. Plumpp was born in Clinton, Mississippi, in 1940 and lived on a tenant farm until 1954. He is presently an Assistant Professor in the Black Studies Program, University of Illinois at Chicago Circle. His books include: *Portable Soul*; *Half Black, Half Blacker*; *Black Rituals*; and *Somehow We Survive* (ed.). *Common Hands*, a volume of revolutionary poetry is forthcoming from Peoples College Press. He has won two Illinois Arts Council Literary Awards for work published in little magazines. He is currently working on a novella about a blues singer, and living with his wife, Falvia, and daughter, Harriet Nzinga, in Chicago.

Also from Thunder's Mouth Press

From Sand Creek, Simon J. Ortiz
She Had Some Horses, Joy Harjo
Somehow We Survive, Sterling D. Plumpp (ed.)